SPEAK

— WITH —

CONFIDENCE

SPEAK
—WITH—
CONFIDENCE

NIDHI SAINI

World Champion of Public Speaking

(Semifinalist)

Worldwide Published by

Pendown Press

PENDOWN PRESS LLP
An ISO 9001 & ISO 14001 Certified Co.,
Regd. Office: 3767A, Kanhaiya Nagar,
Tri Nagar, Delhi-110035
Ph.: 8130886000, 9650072927
E-mail: info@pendownpress.com
Branch Office: 1A/2A, 20, Hari Sadan, Ansari Road,
Daryaganj, New Delhi-110002
Ph.: 011-45794768
Website: PendownPress.com

Edition: 2025
Price: ₹ 399
ISBN: 978-93-6338-540-5

Layout and Cover Designed by Pendown Graphics Team
Printed and Bound in India by Thomson Press India Ltd.

CONTENTS

Acknowledgements — i

Foreword — iii

Praises From the Experts — vi

Preface — v

From Silence to Spotlight — vii
My Story of Authentically Being Me

Chapter 1 — 1
- Understanding the Fear of Public Speaking

Chapter 2 — 11
- Embracing the Power of a Positive Mindset

Chapter 3 — 20
- Setting Your Speaking Goals

Chapter 4 — 27
- Preparing for Success

Chapter 5 — 32
- Mastering the Art of Presentation Design

Chapter 6 — 39
- Practicing Your Delivery

Chapter 7 — 46
- Managing Nervousness and Anxiety

Chapter 8   53

● Building Confidence through Rehearsal

Chapter 9   60

● Engaging Your Audience

Chapter 10   68

● Overcoming Fear & Embracing Fearless Presentation

Conclusion   75

It's Your Time to Take Centre Stage   77

□ □ □ □

ACKNOWLDGEMENTS

Whatever I have achieved in life, would have been impossible without the support of my parents. They've taught me unconditional love and I have seen them grow along with me. The wings that I have today would not have been possible without them. Thank you, Papaji & Mummy, for always having my back. I love you so much.

My son, Pranav, has been my best friend & biggest cheerleader. He is the one who keeps me motivated and encourages me to do my best. Through thick & thin, he has supported me at every step. Thank you beta!

I am hugely indebted to my brother, Nitesh, who has stood by me at every step. He has always guided me and encouraged me to keep moving forward.

Special gratitude to all my friends who have always believed in me and have been my pillars of strength.

I wish to express my gratitude to Toastmasters for giving me a platform to share my voice and stories. My heart is always with my Noida Toastmasters Club, which is my second home and happy place.

My heartfelt gratitude to all my mentors and guides who have shown me light and direction in times of confusion.

I want to thank all my connections who have kept me motivated to do good work and serve them better.

I am thankful to the entire team at Pendown Press for their support and suggestions throughout the creative process.

Huge Gratitude to all with whom my paths have crossed and who have created an impact on my journey.

Thank you all!

FOREWORD

When a powerful speaker like Nidhi decides to share, one is bound to sit up and take notice! "Speak with Confidence" is a unique collection of ideas, both theoretical and practical, that allows the reader to think, prepare, and rehearse for success.

Narrated as the journey of the main protagonist - Riya, the chapters act as a fulcrum that build upon each other to create a cohesive experience that will undoubtedly help one learn, unlearn, and relearn with dexterity.

Be it ways to face glossophobia, the fear of public speaking, embracing the power of having a positive mindset, learning how to effectively set goals for oneself, or preparing for success, the book has a recipe that is sure to help you succeed.

What I also love about this collection of ideas is the real-life applicability of the theories. It will teach you not just about presentation design, but also about how you can overcome your nervousness, build confidence through self-introspective rehearsals, and engage your audience by embracing your flaws.

The perfect job aid for those who seek to speak with confidence and panache – this one is a banger that must be read and re-read!

Ayan Pal,
Strategic Planning & Implementation Consultant
Head, Centre for Advanced Studies, IBM
Author, Readomania
District Director, Toastmasters International (Past)

PRAISES FROM THE EXPERTS

In her book "Speak with Confidence", Nidhi Saini takes the reader on an empowering journey of self-discovery and growth. The book highlights the importance of embracing our imperfections and connecting authentically with our listeners. Through relatable examples, self-reflection exercises, and goal-setting, Nidhi encourages readers to transform their fear into strength by viewing every speaking opportunity as a chance for growth and impact. This makes Nidhi's book ideal for anyone looking to elevate their confidence by owning their story, embracing vulnerability, and believing in themselves.

Manoj Vasudevan
CEO, Thought Expressions
World Champion of Public Speaking, 2017
Leadership Coach

Nidhi is an exceptional person and speaker. I had the pleasure of watching her speak and the 2023 World Semi Finals and loved her ability to be light yet enlightening at the same time. Truly amazing!

I can't think of a better person to support people to speak with confidence, and I love that this book offers so many opportunities to reflect on your own speaking journey as you build your confidence one chapter at a time.

Verity Price
DTM, Accredited Speaker
World Champion of Public Speaking, 2021
Presenting Coach, Cape Town

PREFACE

In the modern world, the ability to communicate effectively is a superpower. It's a skill that can propel careers, inspire change, and connect people in ways that transform lives. Yet, for many, the fear of public speaking stands as a daunting barrier to unlocking this superpower.

This Book, **"Speak with Confidence: Mastering the Art of Public Speaking for the Fearful"** is a beacon of hope for all those who have ever wrestled with their fear of public speaking. Through the inspiring journey of our protagonist, Riya, you will discover that fear is not an insurmountable obstacle but a challenge to be met and managed. You will explore the transformation of a timid, anxious speaker into a confident, fearless presenter, and you will realize that this journey is one you can embark on too.

Fear of public speaking is a shared experience, transcending borders and cultures. It's a universal challenge that can be met with universal solutions. The journey you are about to embark upon is not just about learning techniques but about embarking on a path of self-discovery and personal growth. It's about nurturing the skills to captivate and connect with your audience, to make a lasting impact, and to leave a legacy through your words.

As you delve into the journey of Riya, you'll uncover invaluable insights, practical strategies, and interactive exercises to help you confront your fear of public speaking head-on. You'll learn the art of crafting compelling content, perfecting your delivery, and managing nervousness. You'll even grasp the importance of audience engagement and discover the power of a positive mindset.

This is not just a book; it's a journey, and I encourage you to embrace it with an open heart. With every chapter, you'll grow one step closer to becoming a fearless presenter, one who can confidently and authentically share their message with the world.

Whether you're a working professional, a business owner, a seasoned speaker looking to enhance your skills, or someone who's just starting out this book is here to guide you. May it be a source of inspiration, empowerment, and the tools you need to unlock your inner speaker.

Your voice is unique and powerful. It deserves to be heard.

Good Luck & Bon Voyage!

FROM SILENCE TO SPOTLIGHT
My Story of Being Authentically Me

I was born into a typical North Indian family where protectiveness and restrictions were the norm. Naturally, I grew up as a rebel - but one riddled with self-doubt.

All I wanted was to be seen, to be noticed. To achieve that, I resorted to all kinds of silly tactics. Soon enough, I realized I was being noticed - but for all the wrong reasons.

As I grew older, I noticed something else: I had no specific passion, except for this relentless desire to be seen. I loved being on stage but didn't want to put in the effort to speak. I wanted the glory without the grind. I wanted heaven without dying. So, whenever I found myself on stage, I chose to stay silent or speak as little as possible.

The easy way out? Dance groups or theatre. In school and college, I'd be on stage to perform or act in mime but never to speak.

In fact, I even lost the election for Vice President of my college Dramatics Society simply because I couldn't pitch myself.

Speaking felt like a mountain I wasn't ready to climb.

Thankfully, by my third year, I managed—yes, managed—to become the President.

But my struggles with speaking weren't over. During my post-graduate dissertation presentation, I was a complete disaster.

I didn't even consider speaking as a skill I could develop - it was something I avoided entirely. And yet, I walked around confidently, hiding behind a facade.

Have you heard of Imposter Syndrome? That was me - faking my way through, terrified of being exposed.

Life was cruising along until it hit turbulence. At 33, I walked out of my marriage, with my 5-year-old son. Life demanded that I play multiple roles - protector, provider, and parent. Every day felt like a battlefield. Some days, I was a warrior; other days, I was a wounded soldier, battered by my own self-doubt.

And speaking? Still far from my mind.

But looking back, I realize now that speaking is deeply connected to our inner selves.

When life cracked open and midlife crisis crept in, I found myself questioning everything.

After 15 years in a profession I'd studied for, I decided to hang up my boots and start fresh. This decision marked the beginning of my new life - and a journey towards discovering my purpose. I became an educator and, for the first time, felt a sense of contentment and joy.

Teaching wasn't just a job - it was a calling.

It was here that I began to understand the true power of communication. My role wasn't just about sharing knowledge, it was about *connecting with people, building trust, and making an impact.*

This realization spurred me to study more. I pursued an M.Sc. in Psychology and completed CELTA from Cambridge University and the British Council.

By 2018, I had branched out as an independent ESL trainer, working with leading EdTech companies in India. Things were great until I hit a new crossroads.

I was working with CEOs and senior leaders - people who were at the peak of their professional success - only to find they were plagued by hesitation and low confidence, especially when it came to speaking English. Their vulnerability shocked me.

These were accomplished individuals who felt small simply because they couldn't express themselves fluently.

One day, a company Founder said to me, "Nidhi Ma'am, you speak so well. I can't even talk to my team properly. Look at others, they're so much better than me."

That hit me hard. Why should language, or the lack of it, define someone's confidence?

That moment marked a turning point.

I decided to move beyond teaching English and focus on something bigger: building confidence as a speaker and communicator.

And so began a new chapter in my life as a Communication Skills and Public Speaking Coach.

But life wasn't done testing me yet. Certain devastating events in my life hit me hard. I soon found myself in a dark emotional spiral, questioning everything about myself. My once unshakable confidence was gone. I felt like a skeleton of who I used to be. I had to make some immediate amends to move forward.

Professional help and coaching pulled me out of that darkness, helping me rebuild my self-esteem, one brick at a time.

And that's when I had my epiphany: if I could lose confidence despite my resilience, there must be so many others out there struggling silently. My mess became my message. I started sharing my story online and in my sessions. What began as casual sharing quickly turned into something more - a source of inspiration for many.

In 2021, I joined Toastmasters. Little did I know this would become a life-changing journey. Toastmasters helped me refine my craft and gave me the stage I once dreamt of yet silently feared all through.

But I had now learned to face my fears. In 2023, I became the first and only woman to represent India on the global stage at the World Championship of Public Speaking. My Josh Talk has garnered over 2.5 million views as we speak. I've received accolades and awards—but more importantly, **I've discovered the power of being myself.**

From a rebellious teenager who was obsessed with being seen (without any purpose) to a 48-year-old who speaks confidently with purpose & is now helping others transform - life has been my biggest teacher.

People ask me why did I choose this work. My answer is that *I didn't choose my work, my work chose me.*

The reason I am sharing this is to share with you the biggest secret to speaking successfully and fearlessly right at the beginning of this book.

Before we move forward to understanding and mastering the psychology, tools, and exercises that are guaranteed to shift you from being a nervous speaker to a notable one, the learning you need to take from my story is this one truth bomb.

Here's the truth: the secret to speaking well is simply this - **BE YOURSELF**. Own your story, embrace your vulnerability, and believe in who you are.

Speaking isn't just about technique; it's about connection. And that's what I help people do - connect with themselves and their audience.

This book is intended to take you through that journey of self-discovery and show you how to harness the power of being YOU to be a Better SPEAKER.

Speak & Shine my friend!.

CHAPTER - 1

UNDERSTANDING THE FEAR OF PUBLIC SPEAKING

Riya's Journey from **Pain to Fearlessness**

As you open this first chapter of "Speak with Confidence," I invite you to join Riya on her transformative journey from crippling fear to unwavering confidence in public speaking.

Riya's story, like many of us, starts with the pain of paralyzing fear, but it's a journey that holds the promise of becoming a fearless presenter.

I am certain that the majority of you will relate to and empathize with the crippling fear of public speaking/presenting that doesn't allow us to shine at our brightest even though we may be brilliant leaders or team members and absolute masters at what we do. I have been there as you all know from my story in the previous chapter.

So, hold my hand, and together, let's step into Riya's shoes and learn to overcome the hurdles to shining center stage and being seen and heard as we all deserve.

Riya came to me when she found herself at the crossroads of her professional journey. There was a lot of turmoil that was burning her from within and slowly it was diminishing her flame. Let's go back in time and travel alongside Riya.

Meet Riya, a brilliant software engineer based in Mumbai, India, known for her technical prowess and problem-solving skills. However, there's one thing that has always held her back in her professional life - the fear of public speaking.

Riya's fear is not just a little nervousness; it's a paralyzing dread that keeps her up at night before an important presentation. She often recalls a particularly traumatic experience in college when her voice cracked in the middle of a presentation, leaving her feeling humiliated in front of her peers.

That single incident cast a long shadow over her career. In office meetings and presentations, Riya's heart would race, her voice would tremble, and her palms would sweat. The weight of judgment and the fear of failure made every speaking opportunity a living nightmare. The agony of fearing public speaking was so unbearable that it became the stumbling block in her career.

Decoding the Fear

Well, it was time to PAUSE and ask a simple, yet powerful question. -

why after being, a successful software engineer do I feel this way?

The answer indeed is not that simple.

Riya's fear is not unique; it's deeply rooted in human psychology.

We, humans, are a lot dependent on group acceptance and validation for survival, and speaking in front of a group often meant being judged, which could affect one's place in the community.

The fear of public speaking is, in essence, a survival instinct gone awry. It's not a weakness; it's a part of our evolutionary heritage.

When you understand this, it can be the first step in breaking free from the prison of fear.

As Riya delves into understanding her fear, she learns about its personal triggers. She realizes that past failures, criticism, or embarrassing moments are like ghosts that haunt her confidence. They need to be acknowledged and exorcised to move forward.

Furthermore, Riya struggles **with the fear of the unknown.**

Stepping onto a stage or in front of an audience means facing unfamiliar faces, unpredictable reactions, and the potential for vulnerability. With practice and preparation, this fear can be harnessed and turned into a source of strength.

For Riya, the fear of public speaking is also linked to the fear of making mistakes.

The pressure to be perfect creates performance anxiety, making every presentation a high-stakes event. But Riya, like anyone, isn't perfect, and it's okay to make mistakes. It's how you respond to them that matters.

The Journey Starts...

As we move forward, you'll accompany Riya as she conquers her fear step by step. We'll explore various strategies and exercises that will help Riya, and you, turn fear into a source of strength and inspiration. The journey to fearlessness begins with this understanding.

Are you ready to embark on this transformative journey alongside Riya and countless others who have faced and conquered their fear of public speaking? The adventure starts here, in Chapter 1.

So, stay engaged, take notes, and let's embrace the challenge of understanding our fear of public speaking together.

Riya's journey will inspire you, and the strategies we'll uncover will empower you.

Get ready to unlock your inner speaker and break free from the chains of fear. The adventure begins now!

THROUGH YOUR EYES

Take a moment to summarize your reflections and set an intention for the upcoming chapters. This worksheet is a tool for self-discovery and growth. Revisit it periodically to track your progress and celebrate the achievements on your path to becoming a confident and influential speaker. The adventure has begun, and you're on your way to unlocking your inner speaker!

Reflecting on Personal Experiences

1.1 Recall Your Own Fear(s)

Think about a specific instance where you felt a fear similar to Riya's. What emotions did you experience, and how did it impact your performance?

____

____

____

____

____

____

1.2   Identifying Triggers

Reflect on the triggers of your public speaking fear. Are there specific incidents or situations that amplify your anxiety? Write down the details.

1.3   Recognizing the Pressure for Perfection

Reflect on your own expectations for perfection in public speaking. How does the fear of making mistakes impact your confidence?

____

____

____

____

____

____

____

____

____

____

____

____

____

____

____

____

____

____

1.4 Acknowledging Root Causes

Identify the root causes of your fear of public speaking. Are there past failures, criticisms, or embarrassing moments that still influence your confidence?

____

____

____

____

____

____

____

____

____

____

____

____

____

____

1.5 Pledge for Growth

Write a personal pledge committing to the journey of overcoming your fear of public speaking. What specific steps are you willing to take to transform your fear into strength?

____

____

____

____

____

____

____

____

____

____

____

____

____

____

____

____

____

____

1.6 Setting Goals

Establish short-term and long-term goals for your public speaking journey. These can be related to overcoming specific fears, improving certain skills, or achieving milestones in your progress.

☐ ☐ ☐ ☐

CHAPTER - 2

EMBRACING THE POWER OF A POSITIVE MINDSET

Having delved into the roots of her fear of public speaking, Riya now finds herself standing at the threshold of transformation. With the understanding that her fear is a part of our shared human heritage, she embarks on the next leg of her journey one towards embracing the power of the mind.

The Power of Positivity

As Riya grapples with her fear, she realizes that a significant part of her struggle lies in the way she perceives public speaking. It's not just about delivering information; it's also about engaging, inspiring, and connecting with the audience.

The real transformation begins when she starts seeing speaking opportunities as chances to make a positive impact rather than fearing judgment.

A Growth Mindset

One of the most potent tools in Riya's arsenal is the adoption of a growth mindset. This concept, championed by psychologist Carol Dweck, suggests that our abilities and intelligence are not fixed traits but can be developed through dedication and hard work.

Riya learns that by adopting a growth mindset, she can shift her perspective on public speaking and herself.

It's essential to understand that a positive mindset is not about ignoring your fear but acknowledging it and choosing to move forward despite it.

When Riya starts embracing this new way of thinking, she sees her fear as an opportunity for growth and learning. She no longer views it as an insurmountable obstacle but as a stepping stone towards becoming a fearless speaker.

Shifting Self-Talk

Riya's self-talk plays a crucial role in shaping her mindset. She begins to challenge and reframe her negative self-talk.

Instead of saying, "I'm terrified of speaking in public," **she starts saying,** "I am learning to be more confident in public speaking."

This simple change in self-talk has a profound impact on her mindset.

Visualization and Affirmations

Riya explores visualization and positive affirmations as tools to strengthen her newfound positive mindset. She practices mentally picturing herself speaking confidently and successfully in various scenarios.

We humans love to think of what may go wrong. However, the magic lies in thinking "What if all goes right?" That's what Riya explores.

Visualization helps her build self-assurance and mental resilience. She also crafts affirmations, positive statements she repeats to herself, to reinforce her belief in her abilities.

The Shift Continues...

Riya's journey is a testament to the power of positive thinking and adopting a growth mindset. She's learning that she can rewire her brain to see public speaking not as a source of fear but as an opportunity for growth, learning, and positive impact. She's well on her way to becoming a fearless speaker.

As you embrace the power of a positive mindset alongside Riya, remember that it's a journey, not a destination. Riya's transformation is ongoing, and so is yours.

Stay engaged, keep practicing, and let's move forward to the next chapter of Riya's **journey toward fearless presentations.**

THROUGH YOUR EYES

Take a moment to summarize your reflections and set an intention for the upcoming chapters. This worksheet is a tool for self-discovery and growth. Revisit it periodically to track your progress and celebrate the achievements on your path to becoming a confident and influential speaker. The adventure has begun, and you're on your way to unlocking your inner speaker!

Reflecting on Personal Experiences

2.1   Identifying Negative Self-Talk

Recognize instances of negative self-talk related to public speaking. Write down a few examples of phrases that contribute to your negative self-talk.

____

____

____

____

____

2.2 Reframing Self-Talk

Challenge and reframe your negative self-talk. Take one of the negative phrases you identified and rephrase it into a positive, growth-oriented statement.

2.3 Your Current Perception

Consider how you currently perceive public speaking. Is it primarily a source of fear, or do you see it as an opportunity to make a positive impact? Reflect on your current mindset & self-talk.

____

____

____

____

____

____

____

____

____

____

____

____

____

____

____

2.4 Shifting Perspectives

Think about instances where you can shift your perception of speaking opportunities. Write down an instance where a change of perspective could help.

2.5 Crafting Affirmations

Create positive affirmations related to public speaking. These should be short, impactful statements that reinforce your belief in your abilities.

For example, "I am becoming a more confident and influential speaker."

____

____

____

____

____

____

____

____

____

____

____

____

____

____

____

2.6 Daily Positive Practices

Outline practical steps you can take daily to reinforce a positive mindset. This could involve repeating affirmations, engaging in visualization exercises, or challenging negative thoughts.

☐ ☐ ☐ ☐

SETTING YOUR SPEAKING GOALS

By now , Riya has learned to embrace the power of a positive mindset, transforming her perception of public speaking from fear to opportunity. Now, as she continues her journey toward fearless presentations, she discovers the importance of setting clear speaking goals.

By the way, as Riya is moving forward with a clear understanding, her work-life is showing signs of growth too. Now it is time to craft a vision for herself.

The Significance of Goals

➤ Riya realizes that setting speaking goals is like charting a course for her public speaking journey.

➤ Without clear objectives, it's easy to become aimless and lose focus.

➤ Goals give her direction, purpose, and motivation.

➤ They serve as beacons guiding her through the turbulent waters of fear and uncertainty.

The First Step

The first step in setting speaking goals is to identify what you want to achieve with your presentations.

Riya begins by asking herself important questions:

➢ *What are my long-term objectives as a speaker?*

➢ *What specific improvements do I want to make in my public speaking abilities?*

➢ *What opportunities do I want to explore that require better speaking skills?*

For Riya, these questions lead to answers such as wanting to lead team meetings with confidence, deliver impactful client presentations, and eventually become a sought-after speaker in her industry.

SMART Goals

Riya discovers the concept of SMART goals:

S   -   Specific

M   -   Measurable

A   -   Achievable

R   -   Relevant

T   -   Time-bound.

Applying this framework to her public speaking journey, she defines her goals with greater clarity. For instance, she sets a SMART goal of leading at least one client presentation per quarter with minimal anxiety within the next year.

Breaking Down Goals

The process doesn't end with just setting SMART goals. Riya learns to break down these larger goals into smaller, manageable steps. She divides her journey into phases and milestones, each with its own set of objectives.

For her quarterly client presentation goal, Riya divides the process into stages, from thorough research to confident delivery, and practices each step

Riya's Takeaway

By setting clear and SMART speaking goals, Riya gains a sense of purpose and direction in her journey to overcome her fear of public speaking. She knows where she's headed and the steps she needs to take to get there. It's a powerful tool that motivates her to push past her comfort zone and embrace every opportunity to practice and improve.

As you set your own speaking goals, remember that you're not alone in your quest for fearlessness. Just like Riya, you're embarking on a transformative journey that will empower you to become a confident and influential speaker.

Stay focused on your goals, and let's move forward together to the next chapter of your fearless presenter's story.

CHAPTER 3 **WORKSHEET**

T H R O U G H   Y O U R   E Y E S

As you accompany Riya on her journey, it's time to set your own speaking goals. Reflect on your professional aspirations and the opportunities that await you.

With Riya as your inspiration, start by setting a few SMART goals related to public speaking. Remember, your goals should be:

➤ **Specific:** Clearly define what you want to achieve.

➤ **Measurable:** Determine how you will measure progress.

➤ **Achievable:** Ensure your goals are realistic and attainable.

➤ **Relevant:** Align your goals with your professional objectives.

➤ **Time-bound:** Set a deadline for achieving each goal.

S

M

A

R

T

3.1   Reflection on Professional Aspirations

Consider your long-term objectives as a speaker. Where do you see yourself in your professional life, and how does public speaking play a role in achieving those aspirations?

____

____

____

____

____

____

____

____

____

____

____

____

____

____

____

____

3.2 Specific Improvements

Identify specific improvements you want to make in your public speaking abilities. Are there areas such as confidence, articulation, or engagement that you aim to enhance?

____

____

____

____

____

____

____

____

____

____

____

____

____

□ □ □ □

CHAPTER - 4

PREPARING FOR SUCCESS

Riya has come a long way in her quest to become a fearless presenter. First, she understood the root cause of her fears, then she embraced a positive mindset and set clear speaking goals. Now, as she advances in her journey, she focuses on the vital aspect of preparation. As the wise say, preparation is the key to success. In this chapter, Riya discovers the significance of thorough research and effective content crafting in conquering her fear of public speaking.

The Importance of Preparation

Riya understands that effective preparation is like building a sturdy bridge between her message and her audience. **The more thorough her preparation, the more confident and competent she started to feel as a speaker.** She begins to see preparation as a powerful tool to mitigate her fear of speaking in public.

Thorough Research is KEY

For Riya, research is the cornerstone of her presentation preparation.

She explores various strategies for conducting in-depth research, such as:

1. **Understanding the Audience:** Riya learns to tailor her content to the specific needs, interests, and knowledge

level of her audience. By connecting with her audience's expectations, she makes her presentations more engaging and relevant.

2. **Gathering Credible Sources:** Riya discovers the importance of using trustworthy sources to back her claims and arguments. She has become adept at finding and citing authoritative references to enhance her credibility.

3. **Keeping Up to Date:** Riya realizes the importance of staying current in her industry and field. This ongoing education ensures her content is relevant and up-to-date, instilling confidence in her audience.

Effective Content Crafting

As Riya continues her journey, she hones her skills in content crafting. She learns to structure her presentations logically, ensuring a smooth flow of ideas. Some key elements of effective content crafting she focuses on include:

1. **Clear Message:** Riya identifies the core message of her presentation, ensuring that it's succinct, powerful, and easy for the audience to grasp.

2. **Engaging Storytelling:** She explores the art of storytelling, infusing her presentations with relatable anecdotes and narratives to captivate her audience.

3. **Visual Aids:** Riya understands the impact of visual aids, such as well-designed slides, which complement her spoken words and enhance audience engagement.

4. **Smooth Transitions:** She practices seamless transitions between different sections of her presentation, maintaining a coherent and organized structure.

Riya's Takeaway

So you see, Riya has gained a deeper appreciation for the value of thorough research and effective content crafting.

She's learned that her preparation is not just about combating fear but also about delivering content that resonates with her audience.

As you apply these lessons to your own journey, remember that the more you invest in preparation, the more confident and capable you become as a speaker.

With each step, Riya is moving closer to becoming a fearless presenter. By understanding the importance of research and content crafting, you, too, are on a path to confidently sharing your knowledge, insights, and stories with the world. Prepare thoroughly, and let's continue this journey toward fearless presentations together.

Are you Ready to move closer to your journey to becoming a fearless presenter? If YES, then keep moving further.

PS: Oh yes! Just for clarity, when I say presentation, I do not mean a PowerPoint presentation. It can be any kind of speaking engagement, with or without a ppt.

THROUGH YOUR EYES

Summarize your reflections and intentions for improvement. Remember that preparation is a journey, and each step you take toward mastering the art of preparation brings you closer to becoming a fearless presenter. Stay committed, invest in thorough research, and let's continue this journey toward fearless presentations together.

Reflecting on Your Approach

4.1   Tailoring to Audience Needs

Reflect on how well you currently tailor your content to the needs, interests, and knowledge level of your audience. Identify one area where you can improve in this aspect.

____

____

____

____

____

____

____

____

____

____

____

____

____

4.2 Staying Current

Reflect on your commitment to staying current in your industry or field. How do you ensure your content remains relevant and up-to-date? Identify one action you can take to enhance your ongoing education.

____

____

____

____

____

____

____

____

____

____

____

____

☐ ☐ ☐ ☐

CHAPTER - 5

MASTERING THE ART OF PRESENTATION DESIGN

As Riya progresses on her journey to fearless presentations, she now finds herself delving into the art of presentation design. At this step, she discovers the significance of creating engaging visuals to complement her message. With every slide, she's learning to captivate her audience's attention and make a lasting impact.

The Power of Visuals

Riya realizes that her work involves a lot of team and client presentations, which she always struggled with. She recognizes that effective presentation design is not just about aesthetics; it's about enhancing the audience's comprehension and retention of the content.

Engaging visuals can break down complex ideas, create emotional connections, and make her presentations memorable. For her, mastering presentation design is a crucial step in her quest for fearlessness.

Effective Content Crafting

1. **Clarity and Simplicity:** Riya understands that simplicity is the ultimate sophistication. She learns to create clean, uncluttered slides with a focus on clear, concise content. A

clutter-free slide can help her audience concentrate on her message.

2. **Visual Hierarchy:** Riya explores the concept of visual hierarchy, which involves emphasizing important elements on her slides. She uses size, color, and positioning to guide her audience's attention to the most critical information.

3. **Consistency:** She realizes that maintaining a consistent design style throughout her presentation enhances its professional look and keeps the audience engaged. Consistency includes using the same fonts, colors, and slide layouts.

4. **Storytelling through Visuals:** Riya discovers the power of using images and graphics to tell a compelling story. Visuals can create emotional connections and convey complex concepts more effectively than text alone.

5. **Minimal Text, Maximum Impact:** She practices minimizing the amount of text on her slides, opting for bullet points or concise phrases. This forces her to speak to the content rather than reading slides verbatim.

Riya's Takeaway

With each slide she creates, Riya becomes more proficient in the art of presentation design.

She's learning that visuals are not just a supplement to her message; they are an integral part of how she communicates with her audience.

As you apply these lessons to your own journey, remember that engaging visuals can significantly impact the effectiveness of your presentations.

Mastering presentation design is another step in Riya's transformation into a fearless presenter. By creating slides that are clear, consistent, and visually appealing, she's moving closer to becoming an influential speaker.

As you learn to captivate your audience through your visuals, you, too, will progress on your path to fearless presentations. Design your slides thoughtfully, and let's continue this journey together.

THROUGH YOUR EYES

Summarize your reflections and intentions for improvement. Remember that preparation is a journey, and each step you take toward mastering the art of preparation brings you closer to becoming a fearless presenter. Stay committed, invest in thorough research, and let's continue this journey toward fearless presentations together.

Reflecting on Your Approach

5.1 Current Approach to Visual Elements

Consider how you currently approach the visual elements of your presentation slides. Are they cluttered or clear, consistent or haphazard? Reflect on the strengths and areas for improvement in your current practices.

____

____

____

____

____

____

____

____

____

____

____

____

5.2 Effective Use of Visuals

Are your visuals enhancing comprehension and retention?
Identify one visual element you believe works well and one that
might need improvement.

____

____

____

____

____

____

____

____

____

____

____

5.3 Goals for Visual Enhancement

Jot down specific goals for enhancing the visual elements of your presentations. These could be related to simplicity, visual hierarchy, consistency, storytelling, or minimizing text.

5.4 Implementation Plan

Outline a plan for implementing the strategies you've identified. What steps will you take to incorporate these enhancements into your future presentations?

____

____

____

____

____

____

____

____

____

____

____

____

□ □ □ □

CHAPTER - 6

PRACTICING YOUR DELIVERY

By now Riya arrives at a crucial juncture – the practice of effective delivery. This definitely is the most dreadful juncture for her. Do you remember when I mentioned at the start, that Riya trembled at the thought of speaking and her voice would choke?

This was the testing phase for her. Now Riya was ready to focus on refining her tone, pacing, and body language, ultimately gaining the confidence to speak in public with grace and poise. Let's catch up with her on this journey.

The Power of Effective Delivery

Riya understands that the best-crafted content and visuals are only as impactful as the way they're delivered.

Effective delivery goes beyond what you say; it's about how you say it. By mastering the nuances of vocal expression and body language, Riya is learning to engage her audience and command the stage.

Techniques for Effective Delivery

1. **Voice Modulation:** Riya recognizes the significance of modulating her voice. She practices varying her tone, pitch, and volume to convey emotion and emphasize key points. She learns that a monotone delivery can be boring and disengaging for the audience.

2. **Pacing and Pause:** Riya appreciates the power of pacing and strategic pauses. She experiments with speaking at a comfortable speed and strategically inserting pauses to allow her audience to absorb information and build anticipation.

3. **Confidence in Non-Verbal Cues:** Body language plays a critical role in Riya's delivery. She learns that open and confident posture, appropriate gestures, and maintaining eye contact with her audience help convey assurance and establish a connection.

4. **Practice, Practice, Practice:** Riya understands that practice is the key to perfecting her delivery. She rehearses her presentations multiple times, recording herself to review and refine her speaking style.

Riya's Takeaway

Riya discovers that effective delivery is a key component of confident public speaking. She realizes that what she says is just as important as how she says it. When she focused on these little aspects, her nervousness was vanishing. She realizes that the fear is also stemming from her unpreparedness for her presentations. The moment she starts paying attention to little details and puts them into practice, she notices becoming confident.

As you apply these lessons to your own journey, remember that your voice and body language are powerful tools for conveying confidence and engaging your audience.

Practicing delivery is another step in Riya's transformation into a fearless presenter. By mastering her tone, pacing, and body language, she's gaining the confidence to command the stage.

As you refine your delivery skills, you, too, are progressing on your path to fearless presentations. Practice your delivery thoughtfully, and let's continue this journey together.

THROUGH YOUR EYES

Summarize your reflections and intentions for improvement. Remember that preparation is a journey, and each step you take toward mastering the art of preparation brings you closer to becoming a fearless presenter. Stay committed, invest in thorough research, and let's continue this journey toward fearless presentations together.

Reflecting on Your Approach

6.1 Voice Modulation

Reflect on how you currently modulate your voice. Are you varying your tone, pitch, and volume to convey emotion and emphasize key points? Identify one area for improvement in your voice modulation.

____

____

____

____

____

____

6.2 Body Language Awareness

Reflect on your awareness of body language while speaking. Are you mindful of your posture, gestures, and eye contact? Identify one aspect of your body language that you can enhance to convey more confidence.

6.3 Areas for Enhancement

Jot down specific areas of your delivery style that you would like to enhance. These could be related to voice modulation, pacing, pauses, or body language.

____

____

____

____

____

____

____

____

____

____

____

____

____

6.4 Techniques to Implement

Outline the techniques you plan to implement to enhance your delivery. Be specific about how you will practice and incorporate these improvements into your presentations.

____

____

____

____

____

____

____

____

____

____

____

____

____

☐ ☐ ☐ ☐

CHAPTER - 7

MANAGING NERVOUSNESS AND ANXIETY

Riya's quest for speaking fearlessly has been a journey of self-discovery and skill development. Till now you've seen how she focused on mastering the delivery of her presentations. **Now, she finds herself further confronting one of her most persistent challenges: managing nervousness and anxiety.**

Riya is now ready to explore strategies for staying calm and confident when facing her fear of public speaking.

The Prevalence of Nervousness

As Riya delves into managing nervousness and anxiety, she comes to understand that these emotions are not unique to her. In fact, many accomplished speakers and performers experience them. She realized that the key is not to eliminate these feelings but to harness and channel them in a positive way.

Riya learns the importance of breathing and relaxation techniques in calming her nerves. She practices deep breathing exercises that help reduce physical tension and anxiety. She discovers that simply taking a few moments to breathe deeply before stepping onto the stage or in front of an audience, can be a powerful tool for staying composed.

Visualization & Positive Self-Talk

Visualization and positive self-talk are other methods that Riya discovers and embraces. Until now Riya used to visualize only what could go wrong. But now she visualizes herself delivering a successful presentation, which boosts her confidence and lessens her anxiety. She also develops a set of positive affirmations that she repeats to herself before speaking, reinforcing her belief in her abilities.

She finds a magic wand that can now be used whenever she wants.

Familiarization and Rehearsal Breathing & Relaxation Techniques

Riya learns the importance of breathing and relaxation techniques in calming her nerves.

One of the most effective ways to manage nervousness is through familiarization and rehearsal. Riya practices her presentations multiple times, often in the actual presentation space when possible. This allows her to get comfortable with her surroundings and reduce her fear of the unknown.

Riya's Takeaway

Managing nervousness is another significant step in Riya's transformation into a fearless presenter. **Riya discovers that managing nervousness and anxiety is not about erasing these emotions but harnessing them in a positive way. She's learning to use techniques like deep breathing, visualization, and positive self-talk to stay calm and confident when speaking.**

As you apply these lessons to your own journey, remember that nervousness is a common experience shared by many. By practicing these strategies, you can transform anxiety into a source of energy and focus, allowing you to deliver presentations with confidence and poise.

Stay committed to managing your nervousness, and let's continue this journey together.

THROUGH YOUR EYES

Summarize your reflections and intentions for improvement. Remember that preparation is a journey, and each step you take toward mastering the art of preparation brings you closer to becoming a fearless presenter. Stay committed, invest in thorough research, and let's continue this journey toward fearless presentations together.

Reflecting on Your Approach

7.1   Identification

Reflect on your own experiences with nervousness and anxiety when speaking in public. How do these emotions manifest for you? Are there specific physical sensations or thoughts that you associate with fear? Take a moment to jot down your own experiences and feelings and what triggers them.

____

____

____

____

____

7.2 Identified Strategies

Jot down the specific strategies from breathing techniques, visualization, positive affirmations, and rehearsal that resonate with you the most.

7.3 Implementation Plan

Specify when and how you will incorporate these strategies to manage nervousness effectively.

____

____

____

____

____

____

____

____

____

____

____

____

☐ ☐ ☐ ☐

CHAPTER - 8

BUILDING CONFIDENCE THROUGH REHEARSAL

Riya's pursuit of fearless presentations has taken her through an enlightening journey of self-discovery and skill development. Having explored strategies for managing nervousness and anxiety, she now finds herself at a pivotal stage in her transformation: the process of building confidence through rehearsal.

Can you recall your parents or grandparents or a teacher telling you that **'Practice makes Perfect'**?

I am certain that we all have

heard it at one time or another. So, of course, Riya has heard it too and comprehends the wisdom behind this is not to be ignored.

The Significance of Rehearsal

Riya recognizes that rehearsal is the linchpin of her journey. It's the practice that allows her to fine-tune her content, delivery, and overall presentation. By rehearsing thoroughly and systematically, she builds the confidence she needs to face her fear of public speaking head-on.

Practical Exercises for Effective Rehearsal that Helped Riya

1. **Mock Presentations:** Riya engages in mock presentations. She practices in front of a trusted friend, family member, or even a mirror. This offers the opportunity to receive constructive feedback and improvise the act of presenting.

2. **Recording and Self-Review:** Riya uses technology to record her practice sessions. She's able to evaluate her performance and identify areas that need improvement. It's a powerful tool for honing her delivery and content, along with doing self-reflection

3. **Timing and Pacing:** Timing is crucial in presentations. Riya practices her pacing to ensure she doesn't rush or drag out her speech. She uses a timer to keep her presentation within the allotted time.

4. **Handling Q&A:** To prepare for audience questions, Riya practices answering potential queries related to her presentation. This rehearsal ensures she's poised and confident during the Q&A session. For this she assumes the kind of questions or objections, the audience could ask and practices accordingly. This helps her wonderfully.

Riya's Takeaway

Through this lap of her journey, Riya discovers that building confidence through rehearsal is not about memorizing every word but about familiarizing herself with the content and the act of presenting. She's learning that practice makes perfect, and the more she rehearses, the more confident and competent she becomes as a speaker.

She understands that looking effortless depends on the effort she puts behind the scenes. It's the art of discipline.

As you apply these lessons to your own journey, remember that rehearsal is the key to fearlessness. By practicing your content, delivery, and handling of audience questions, you gain the confidence to face any audience with poise and assurance.

Building confidence through rehearsal is another essential step in Riya's transformation into a fearless presenter. To be fearless, stay committed to your rehearsal process, and let's continue this journey together.

THROUGH YOUR EYES

By reflecting on and refining your rehearsal process, you're actively contributing to your journey toward fearless presentations. Building confidence through rehearsal is a continuous process, and each practice session is a step closer to mastery. For now, it's time to Reflect!

Reflection on Current Rehearsal Practices

8.1 Current Rehearsal Process

How do you typically practice for presentations? Are there specific methods you find effective, or do you face challenges in your current approach?

____

____

____

____

____

____

____

____

____

____

____

____

____

____

____

____

8.2 Personal Confidence Level

Assess your current confidence level when it comes to public speaking. On a scale of 1 to 10, where do you currently place yourself? What are your reasons for this rating?

____

____

____

____

____

Interactive Application

8.3 Techniques Adoption

Choose one or more rehearsal techniques from Riya's journey that resonate with you. How do you plan to incorporate these into your own rehearsal routine?

8.4 Tracking Progress

Create a system to track your progress. This could include keeping a journal or a checklist of key areas to focus on. Regularly review and adjust your approach based on your evolving needs.

____

____

____

____

____

____

____

____

____

____

____

□ □ □ □

CHAPTER - 9

ENGAGING YOUR AUDIENCE

Captivating & Connecting with Confidence

No matter how perfect your content and delivery, communication is only effective when the audience can receive and absorb it. Riya thoroughly gets this. Till now her journey has been an inspiring one of self-discovery and skill development. Having mastered the art of practice and built her confidence, she now reaches another pivotal stage in her transformation: *the ability to engage her audience with confidence.*

The Importance of Audience Engagement

Have you ever attended a presentation where the speaker is the only one talking, with no engagement with the audience? How does it feel? I am sure you might have felt ignored, aloof, disengaged, distracted, unimportant, or lost. That's what happens when you as an audience are not involved.

Riya understands that the true impact of a presentation lies in her ability to captivate and connect with the audience. Engaging her audience is not just about delivering information; it's about creating a memorable and meaningful experience. Now she finds herself ready to understand this aspect of her speaking journey.

Effective Techniques for Audience Engagement

1. **Relatable Storytelling:** Riya embraces the art of storytelling, using relatable anecdotes and narratives to draw her audience into her presentation. She understands that stories create emotional connections and make content memorable. Something that she understands clearly is that stories can be any example, anecdote, comparison, incident, or event that supports her message. Understanding this made creating content easier for her.

2. **Interactive Elements:** Riya experiments with interactive elements, such as asking questions, group discussions, random objects, and polls, to involve her audience actively in her presentation. Eye Contact and Connection: Riya practices maintaining eye contact with her audience, creating a personal connection. She learns quick tricks to establish rapport and convey confidence. Understanding how she can create eye contact so that it doesn't make her awkward, was the key. Finding those 2-5 people across the room, to have eye contact with, really enabled her.

3. **Adding Humour:** Riya has a funny bone that would get lost when she had to speak. She understands how using her natural knack for humour can help her connect with the audience.

Riya's Learning

Through this lap, Riya discovers the power of engaging her audience. She's learning that audience engagement is not just about her words but also about what she does to connect with those listening to her. Interaction fosters engagement and helps retain the audience's attention have been her biggest learnings.

As you apply these lessons to your own journey, remember that captivating and connecting with your audience is within your reach, regardless of your fear of public speaking. You have the ability to create memorable and meaningful experiences for your audience. Stay committed to engaging your audience, and let's continue this journey together.

THROUGH YOUR EYES

By reflecting on and refining your rehearsal process, you're actively contributing to your journey toward fearless presentations. Building confidence through rehearsal is a continuous process, and each practice session is a step closer to mastery. For now, it's time to Reflect!

Reflection on Current Rehearsal Practices

9.1 Current Engagement Practices

Reflect on your current strategies for audience engagement in your presentations. How do you typically capture and maintain your audience's attention? Are there specific techniques you currently use?

____

____

____

____

____

____

9.2 Challenges in Engagement

Identify any challenges you face in engaging your audience. Are there aspects of audience interaction or connection that you find particularly challenging?

9.3 Engagement Goals

Establish specific goals for audience engagement in your future presentations. What outcomes do you hope to achieve by implementing these techniques?

____

____

____

____

____

____

____

____

____

____

____

____

____

____

9.4 Continuous Improvement

Develop a plan for continuous improvement, including seeking
feedback, attending workshops, or exploring new engagement
techniques.

____

____

____

____

____

____

____

____

____

____

____

☐ ☐ ☐ ☐

CHAPTER - 10

OVERCOMING FEAR & EMBRACING FEARLESS PRESENTATION

As Riya approaches the final lap of her transformative journey, she stands at the precipice of becoming a fearless presenter. She's acquired a wealth of knowledge and skills, and her path has been marked with self-discovery, determination, and resilience. Now, Riya confronts her fear and is ready to embrace it.

The Moment of Truth

By now Riya recognizes that the fear of public speaking is a formidable adversary, deeply ingrained in her psyche. It's not something that can be eradicated but something that can be managed and transformed into a source of strength. The moment of truth has arrived, and Riya is ready to confront her fear.

Harnessing Fear

Riya learns that the adrenaline rush and nervousness she experiences before a presentation are not weaknesses but signs that she cares about her message and her audience. She discovers that she can harness this energy and channel it into enthusiasm, passion, and focus.

Accepting Imperfection

Perfection can never be achieved and this is one lesson Riya understands. She realizes that her perfect was never enough for others and vice-versa. It's so subjective. She understands that it's important to do it rather than just trying to wait for a perfect moment.

Riya understands that no one is perfect, and even the most accomplished speakers make mistakes. **She's learned that it's not about being flawless but about being authentic** She accepts imperfection as part of the human experience.

Visualizing Success

Visualization has become a powerful tool for Riya. She imagines herself stepping onto the stage with confidence, speaking passionately, and connecting with her audience. This mental rehearsal boosts her self-assurance and minimizes fear.

Embracing the Journey

Riya acknowledges that the journey to fearless presentations is ongoing. It's not a destination but a continuous process of growth and improvement. She knows that each presentation is an opportunity to learn and refine her skills.

Riya's Triumph

By now when Riya turns around to see how far she's come, it's a moment of pride and contentment. She's learned to harness her fear, embrace her imperfections, and visualize success. She feels empowered and knows she's in control of her emotions.

And my dear fearless presenters, as you apply these lessons to your own journey, remember that fear is a challenge to be managed, not a barrier that cannot be overcome.

Riya's journey is an inspiring testament to the power of determination and self-discovery. By following in her footsteps, you, too, can become a fearless presenter. Your journey may be ongoing, but every step you take brings you closer to confidently sharing your message and making a positive impact on your audience.

Stay committed to confronting your fear and embracing the path to fearless presentations. The journey is yours to embrace, and I'm here to support you every step of the way

THROUGH YOUR EYES

By reflecting on your fear, learning from Riya's journey, and committing to growth, you're actively working towards becoming a fearless presenter. Remember that the journey is ongoing, and each step brings you closer to confidently sharing your message. Stay committed, embrace the process, and know that you're not alone on this journey.

Reflecting on Your Fear

10.1 Fear Reflection

Take a moment to reflect on your fear of public speaking. How has it influenced your presentations and your overall attitude toward public speaking? Be honest about the emotions and challenges you've faced.

____

____

____

____

____

____

10.2 Approaches to Fear

Consider the strategies you've used to manage your fear. What has worked well for you, and what hasn't? Reflect on any patterns associated with your fear.

Commitment to Growth

10.3 Personal Commitment

Declare your commitment to confronting your fears and embracing the path to fearless presentations outlining your dedication to personal growth in public speaking.

10.4 Support System

Identify individuals or resources that can support you on your journey. This could include friends, mentors, or public speaking courses. How can you leverage this support system to enhance your skills?

____

____

____

____

____

____

____

____

____

____

□ □ □ □

CONCLUSION
THIS IS THE BEGINNING OF SOMETHING GOOD

As we reach the final pages of this book: I hope you've enjoyed this transformative journey with Riya and have been inspired by her determination and resilience. Fear of public speaking is a common and deeply ingrained challenge, but with the right tools and mindset, it can be conquered.

Throughout this book, you've explored the roots of the fear of public speaking, developed a positive mindset, set clear goals, honed your preparation and design skills, perfected your delivery, learned to manage nervousness, and discovered the power of audience engagement. You've gained valuable insights and techniques to become a confident and fearless presenter.

Remember that becoming a fearless presenter is a process of growth and self-discovery. It's not about eliminating fear but learning to manage and harness it. Imperfections are a part of the journey, and every presentation is an opportunity to learn and improve. As you continue to practice and apply the knowledge and skills you've acquired, you'll find your fear gradually transforming into a source of strength.

I want to extend my heartfelt congratulations to you for embarking on this journey. Your commitment to becoming a fearless presenter is a testament to your passion and dedication. Continue to confront your fear, practice your skills, and embrace every opportunity to present confidently.

Remember, your voice is a powerful tool, and you have the ability to make a lasting impact with your presentations. Keep speaking, keep learning, and keep inspiring others with your message.

Now is your time to go out there and speak fearlessly.

GO WIN IT!!

IT'S YOUR TIME TO TAKE CENTRE STAGE!

Remember, you have the potential to captivate, inspire, and influence with your words. Every great speaker started with a desire to improve. With dedication and practice, you too can become a master of the Art of Public Speaking.

Thank you for joining us on this journey.

Your voice matters, and the world is waiting to hear what you have to say. So, step confidently onto the stage of life, and let your words shape the future.

Wishing you success and fulfillment in all your speaking endeavors!

Website: www.nidhisaini.com

SCAN QR Code to Reach out to me & check

my work on various platforms